CROCHET

Summer Sensations™

General Information

Many of the products used in this pattern book can be purchased from local craft, fabric and variety stores, or from the Annie's Attic Needlecraft Catalog *(see Customer Service information on page 32)*.

Contents

Enchanting

Design by Sandy Scoville

SKILL LEVEL

INTERMEDIATE

FINISHED SIZES

Instructions given fit woman's small; changes for medium and large are in [ ].

FINISHED GARMENT MEASUREMENT

Chest: 32 inches *(small)* [34 inches *(medium)*, 36 inches *(large)*]

MATERIALS

❑ Fine (sport) weight yarn: 840 (1,008, 1,092) yds lavender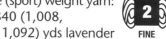
❑ Size G/6/4mm crochet hook or size needed to obtain gauge
❑ Tapestry needle

GAUGE

5 hdc = 1 inch

SPECIAL STITCH

Lover's Knot (LK): Draw up ⅜-inch lp, yo, draw through beg ⅜-inch lp just made, insert hook in lp on left side (not through beg ⅜-inch lp), yo, draw through, yo and draw through 2 lps on hook.

INSTRUCTIONS

Front/Back
Make 2.

Row 1 (RS): Ch 82 [86, 90]; hdc in 3rd ch from hook *(beg 2 sk chs count as a hdc)* and in each rem ch, turn. *(81 [85, 89] hdc)*

Row 2: Ch 2 *(counts as a hdc on this and following rows)*; *hdc in **back lp** *(see Stitch Guide)* of next hdc, hdc in **front lp** *(see Stitch Guide)* of next hdc; rep from * to last hdc and beg 2 sk chs; hdc in back lp of next hdc, hdc in front lp of 2nd ch of beg 2 sk chs, turn.

Row 3: Ch 2; *hdc in back lp of next hdc, hdc in front lp of next hdc; rep from * to last hdc and turning ch-2; hdc in back lp of next hdc, hdc in front lp of 2nd ch of turning ch-2, turn.

Rep row 3 until piece measures approximately 12 [12, 13] inches from beg, ending by working a WS row.

Armhole shaping
Row 1 (RS): Sl st in first 6 hdc; ch 2, continuing in alternating lp pat, hdc in next 68 [72, 76] hdc; **hdc dec** (see Stitch Guide) in next 2 hdc, turn, leaving rem hdc unworked. (70 [74, 78] hdc)

Row 2: Ch 2, continuing in alternating lp pat, hdc in each hdc to beg ch-2, turn, leaving beg ch unworked. (69 [73, 77] hdc)

Row 3: Ch 2, continuing in alternating lp pat, hdc in each hdc and in 2nd ch of turning ch-2, turn.

Rows 4–16: Rep row 3.

Left shoulder & neckline shaping
Row 1 (RS): Ch 2, continuing in pat, hdc in next 23 [27, 31] hdc; dec, turn, leaving rem hdc unworked. (25 [29, 33] hdc)

Row 2: Ch 2, continuing in alternating lp pat, hdc in each hdc and in 2nd ch of turning ch-2, turn.

Row 3: Ch 2, continuing in alternating lp pat, hdc in each hdc to last 2 hdc; dec, turn, leaving turning ch-2 unworked. (23 [27, 31] hdc)

Rows 4–11: [Work rows 2 and 3] 4 times. (15 [19, 23] hdc at end of row 11)

Rows 12 & 13: Rep row 2.
Fasten off and weave in ends.

Right shoulder & neckline shaping
Hold piece with RS facing you and row 16 at top; sk next 18 [14, 10] unused hdc from Left Shoulder Shaping, join in next hdc.

Row 1 (RS): Ch 2, continuing in alternating lp pat, hdc in each hdc and in 2nd ch of turning ch-2, turn. (25 [29, 33] hdc)

Row 2: Ch 2, continuing in alternating lp pat, hdc in each hdc to last 2 hdc; hdc dec, turn, leaving beg ch-2 unworked. (23 [27, 31] hdc)

Row 3: Ch 2, continuing in alternating lp pat, hdc in each hdc and in 2nd ch of turning ch-2, turn.

Row 4: Ch 2, continuing in alternating lp pat, hdc in each hdc to last 2 hdc; hdc dec, turn, leaving turning ch-2 unworked. (21 [25, 29] hdc)

Rows 5–10: [Work rows 3 and 4] 3 times. (15 [19, 23] hdc at end of row 10)

Rows 11–13: Rep row 3.
Fasten off and weave in ends.

Sleeve
Make 2.
Row 1 (RS): Ch 62 [62, 66]; hdc in 3rd ch from hook (beg 2 sk chs count as a hdc) and in each rem ch, turn. (61 [61, 65] hdc)

Row 2: Ch 2, hdc in back lp of next hdc; *hdc in front lp of next hdc, hdc in back lp of next hdc; rep from * to beg 2 sk chs; hdc in front lp of 2nd ch of beg 2 sk chs, turn.

Row 3: Ch 2, hdc in front lp of first hdc—inc made; hdc in back lp of next hdc; *hdc in front lp of next hdc, hdc in back lp of next hdc; rep from * to turning ch-2; hdc in front lp of 2nd ch of turning ch-2, hdc in back lp of same ch—inc made, turn. (63 [63, 67] hdc)

Row 4: Ch 2, hdc in back lp of first hdc—inc made; hdc in front lp of next hdc; *hdc in back lp of next hdc, hdc in front lp of next hdc; rep from * to turning ch-2; hdc in back lp of 2nd ch of turning ch-2, hdc in front lp of same ch—inc made, turn. (65 [65, 69] hdc)

Rows 5–18 [5–18, 5–16]: [Work rows 3 and 4] 7 [7, 6] times. (93 [93, 93] hdc at end of last row)

Row 19 [19, 17]: Ch 2, hdc in back lp of next hdc; *hdc in front lp of next hdc, hdc in back lp of next hdc; rep from * to turning ch-2; hdc in front lp of 2nd ch of turning ch-2, turn.

Row 20 [20, 18]: Ch 2, hdc in front lp of next hdc; *hdc in back lp of next hdc, hdc in front lp of next hdc; rep from * to turning ch-2; hdc in back lp of 2nd ch of turning ch-2, turn.

Rows 21 & 22 [21 & 22, 19–24]: [Work rows 19 [19, 17] and 20 [20, 18] once [once, twice].
Fasten off and weave in ends.

Assembly
With WS tog and with tapestry needle and long ends, sew shoulder seams. Sew Sleeves to body, matching centers of last Sleeve rows to shoulder seams.
Sew underarm and side seams.

Edgings
Neckline Edging
Rnd 1 (RS): Hold top with RS facing you and neckline at top; make slip knot on hook and join with a sc in 1 shoulder seam; working around neckline, sc in end of each row, in each hdc, and in rem shoulder seam; join in joining sc.

Rnd 2: LK (see Special Stitch); sc in next sc, LK; rep from * around; join in joining sc.
Fasten off and weave in ends.

Sleeve Edging
Hold 1 Sleeve with RS facing you and beg ch at top; make slip knot on hook and join with a sc in underarm seam; working in unused lps of beg ch, LK; sk next lp; *sc in next lp, LK, sk next lp; rep from * around; join in joining sc.
Fasten off and weave in ends.
Rep on other Sleeve.

Lower Edging
Hold top with RS facing you and lower edge at top; make slip knot on hook and join with a sc in 1 side seam; working around lower edge in unused lps of beg ch, LK; sk next lp; *sc in next lp, LK, sk next lp; rep from * around; join in joining sc.
Fasten off and weave in ends. ❑❑

Purely Elegant

Design by Nazanin Fard

SKILL LEVEL

INTERMEDIATE

MATERIALS

- ❑ DMC Senso size 3 crochet cotton (150 yds/50g per ball): 1 ball #1001 white
- ❑ Size 0/2.50mm steel crochet hook or size needed to obtain gauge
- ❑ Tapestry needle
- ❑ Sewing needle and matching thread
- ❑ White V-neck pullover

GAUGE

8 dc = 1 inch

INSTRUCTIONS

Small Motif

Make 2.

First Circle

Ch 6, join to form a ring; ch 3 *(counts as a dc)*, 16 dc in ring; join in 3rd ch of beg ch-3. *(17 dc)*

Fasten off. Mark as first Circle made.

2nd Circle

Ch 6, join to form a ring; ch 3 *(counts as a dc)*, sl st in any dc on First Circle; 16 dc in ring; join in 3rd ch of beg ch-3. Fasten off.

3rd Circle

Ch 6, join to form a ring; ch 3 *(counts as a dc)*, sk next 4 dc from joined dc on 2nd Circle, sl st in next dc, 16 dc in ring; join in 3rd ch of beg ch-3. Fasten off.

4th & 5th Circles

Ch 6, join to form a ring; ch 3 *(counts as a dc)*, sk next 4 dc from joined dc on last Circle made, sl st in next dc, 16 dc in ring; join in 3rd ch of beg ch-3. Fasten off.

6th Circle

Ch 6, join to form a ring; ch 3, sk next 4 dc from joined dc on 5th Circle, sl st in next dc, 5 dc in ring; sl st in 5th dc from joined dc on First Circle, 9 dc in ring; join in 3rd ch of beg ch-3. Fasten off.

Center Joining

Working around inside of ring of joined Circles, join crochet cotton in 2nd dc from joined dc of any Circle; ch 7; sl st in 2nd dc on next Circle, ch 3, sl st in 4th ch of beg ch-7, ch 3; *sl st in 2nd dc on next Circle, ch 3 sl st in same ch on beg ch-7, ch 3; rep from * 3 times; join in same dc as joining sl st made. Fasten off.

Center Daisy

Rnd 1: Ch 6, join to form a ring, ch 3 *(counts as a dc)*, 15 dc in ring, join in 3rd ch of beg ch-3. *(16 dc)*

Rnd 2: *Ch 10, sc in 2nd ch from hook, hdc in next ch, dc in next ch, tr in next 3 chs, dc in next ch, hdc in next ch, sc in next ch—*petal made;* sl st in next dc; rep from * 14 times; ch 10, sc in 2nd ch from hook, hdc in next ch, dc in next ch, tr in next 3 chs, dc in next ch, hdc in next ch, sc in next ch—*petal made;* join in joining sl st. Fasten off. *(16 petals)*

Rnd 3: Join crochet cotton in top of any petal; ch 2, sl st in 5th dc from joining on First Circle of first Small Motif; ch 2, sl st in top of next petal, ch 2, sl st 5th dc from joining on next Circle, ch 2, sl st in top of next petal, [ch 5, sl st in 3rd ch from hook—*picot made;* ch 2, sl st in top of next petal] 9 times; ch 2, sl st in 5th dc from joining on First Circle on 2nd Small Motif; ch 2, sl st in top of next petal, ch 2, sl st in 5th dc from joining on next Circle, ch 2, sl st in top of next petal, [ch 5, picot, ch 2, sl st in top of next petal] twice; ch 5, picot, ch 2; join in joining sl st.

Fasten off and weave in ends.

First Side Daisy

Work same as Center Daisy through rnd 2.

Rnd 3: Join crochet cotton in top of any petal; ch 2, sk next sl st in 5th dc from joining on 5th Circle on first Small Motif; ch 2, sl st in top of next petal, ch 2, sl st in 5th dc from joining on next Circle, ch 2, sl st in top of next petal, [ch 5, sl st in 3rd ch from hook—*picot made;* ch 2, sl st in top of next petal] 13 times; ch 5, picot, ch 2; join in joining sl st. Fasten off.

2nd Side Daisy

Work same as Center Daisy through rnd 2.

Rnd 3: Join crochet cotton in top of any petal; ch 2, sk next sl st in 5th dc from joining on 5th Circle on 2nd Small Motif; ch 2, sl st in top of next petal, ch 2, sl st in 5th dc from joining on next Circle, ch 2, sl st in top of next petal, [ch 5, sl st in 3rd ch from hook—*picot made;* ch 2, sl st in top of next petal] 13 times; ch 5, picot, ch 2; join in joining sl st.

Fasten off and weave in all ends.

Finishing

Referring to photo for placement, arrange motifs along neckline. With sewing needle and matching thread, sew outside edge of motifs to neckline of pullover. ❑❑

Camisole Top

Design by Darla Sims

SKILL LEVEL

INTERMEDIATE

FINISHED SIZES

Instructions given fit woman's small; changes for medium, large and X-large are in [ ].

FINISHED GARMENT MEASUREMENT

Chest: 36 inches *(small)* [40 inches *(medium)*, 44 inches *(large)*, 48 inches *(X-large)*]

MATERIALS

❑ Royale Fashion Crochet size 3 crochet cotton (150 yds per ball): 7 (8, 9, 11) balls #325 tangerine
❑ Size D/3/3.25mm crochet hook or size needed to obtain gauge
❑ Tapestry needle
❑ Sewing needle and matching thread
❑ 2 gold ½-inch-diameter shank ball buttons

GAUGE

5 dc = 1 inch

INSTRUCTIONS

Back

Row 1 (RS): Ch 93 [109, 117, 125]; in 7th ch from hook work (4 dc, ch 2, dc)—*shell made (beg 6 sk chs count as a ch-1 sp, a dc and a ch-1 sp);* *sk next 3 chs, in next ch work (dc, ch 1, 1 dc)—*V-st made;* sk next 3 chs, in next ch work (4 dc, ch 2, dc)—*shell made;* rep from * to last 6 chs; sk next 3 chs, in next ch work (dc, ch 1, dc)—*V-st made;* sk next ch, dc in last ch, turn.

Row 2: Ch 3; *V-st in ch-1 sp of next V-st, shell in ch-2 sp of next shell; rep from * to beg 6 sk chs, sk next ch, dc in next ch, turn.

Row 3: Ch 3; *shell in ch-2 sp of next shell; V-st in ch-1 sp of next V-st; rep from * to turning ch-3; dc in 3rd ch of turning ch, turn.

Rep rows 2 and 3 until piece measures 10 inches in length, ending with a row 3.

Upper back

Row 1: Ch 3; *dc in next dc, sk next ch-1 sp, dc in next 2 dc, in next ch-2 sp and in next 4 dc; rep from * across, turn, leaving turning ch unworked. *(89 [105, 113, 121] dc)*

Row 2: Ch 4 *(counts as a dc and a ch-1 sp);* *sk next dc, dc in next st, ch 1; rep from * to turning ch-3; dc in 3rd ch of turning ch, turn.

Row 3: Ch 3; dc in each dc and in each ch-1 sp, turn. *(89 [105, 113, 121] dc)*

Row 4: Ch 3, dc in each dc and in 3rd ch of turning ch-3, turn.

Rep row 4 until piece measures about 4½ inches above row 2, ending with a RS row.

Fasten off.

Armhole shaping

Hold piece with WS facing you; sk first 7 [13, 14, 16] sts of last row worked; join in next dc.

Row 1: Ch 3, dc in next 74 [78, 84, 88] dc, turn, leaving last 7 [13, 14, 16] sts unworked. *(75 [79, 85, 89] dc)*

Row 2: Ch 3; **dc dec** *(see Stitch Guide)* in next 2 sts; dc in each dc to last 3 sts; dc dec in next 2 sts; dc in 3rd ch of turning ch-3, turn. *(73 [77, 83, 87] dc)*

Row 3: Ch 3, dc in each dc and in 3rd ch of turning ch-3, turn.

Row 4: Ch 3; dc dec; dc in each dc to last 3 dc; dc dec; dc in 3rd ch of turning ch-3, turn. *(71 [75, 81, 85] dc)*

Row 5: Ch 3, dc in each dc and in 3rd ch of turning ch-3, turn.

Row 6: Ch 3; dc dec; dc in each dc to last 3 sts; dc dec; dc in 3rd ch of turning ch-3, turn. *(69 [73, 79, 83] dc)*

Rep row 5 until armhole measures 4 [4½, 5, 5½] inches, ending with a WS row.

Right shoulder shaping

Row 1: Ch 3, dc in next 14 [16, 18, 19] dc, turn, leaving rem sts unworked. *(15 [17, 19, 20] dc)*

Row 2: Ch 3, dc in each dc and in 3rd ch of turning ch-3, turn.

Rep row 2 until armhole measures 8 [8½, 9, 9½] inches.

Fasten off.

Left shoulder shaping

Hold piece with RS facing you; sk next 39 [41, 43, 45] dc from Right Shoulder Shaping, join crochet cotton in next st.

Row 1: Ch 3, dc in next 13 [15, 17, 18] dc and in 3rd ch of turning ch-3, turn. *(15 [17, 19, 20] dc)*

Row 2: Ch 3, dc in each dc and in 3rd ch of turning ch-3, turn.

Rep row 2 until armhole measures 8 [8½, 9, 9½] inches.

Fasten off.

Front

Work as for Back through Armhole Shaping.

Last row: Ch 3, dc in each dc and in 3rd ch of turning ch-3, turn.

Right shoulder shaping

Row 1 (WS): Ch 3; dc in next 17 [18, 20, 21] dc, dc dec; dc in next dc, turn, leaving rem sts unworked.

Row 2 (RS): Ch 3; dc in each dc and in 3rd ch of turning ch-3 turn.

Row 3: Ch 3, dc in each dc to last 3 sts; dc dec; dc in 3rd ch of turning ch-3, turn.

Rows 4–11: [Work rows 2 and 3] 5 times. *(15 [16, 18, 19] dc)*

Rep row 2 until piece measures same as back to shoulder.

Fasten off.

Left shoulder shaping

Hold piece with WS facing you; sk next 27 [29, 31, 33] dc from Right Shoulder Shaping; join crochet cotton in next dc.

Row 1: Ch 3, dc dec; dc in next 17 [18, 20, 21] dc and in 3rd ch of turning

ch-3, turn. *(20 [21, 23, 24] dc)*

Row 2: Ch 3, dc in each dc and in 3rd ch of turning ch-3, turn.

Row 3: Ch 3, dc dec; dc in each rem dc and in 3rd ch of turning ch 3, turn. *(19 [20, 22, 23] dc)*

Rows 4–11: [Rep rows 2 and 3] 5 times. *(15 [16, 18, 19] dc)*

Rep row 2 until piece measures same as right shoulder.

Fasten off.

Assembly

With RS facing you, sew shoulder seams and side seams.

Armhole Edging

Hold piece with RS facing you; join crochet cotton in 1 underarm seam; ch 1, sc in same sp; sc evenly spaced around armhole; join in first sc. Fasten off.

Rep on other armhole.

Lower Edging

Hold piece with RS facing you and lower edge at top; join crochet cotton in 1 side seam.

Rnd 1: Ch 1, sc in same sp; working in unused lps of beg ch, sc in each lp and in next seam; join in first sc.

Rnd 2: Ch 3 *(counts as a dc)*, 2 dc in same sc; 3 dc in each rem sc; join in 3rd ch of beg ch 3. Fasten off.

Neck Edging

Hold piece with RS facing you; join crochet cotton in 1 shoulder seam.

Rnd 1: Ch 1, sc in same sp; sc evenly spaced around neck edge, taking care to keep work flat; join in first sc.

Rnd 2: Ch 3 *(counts as a dc)*, 2 dc in same sc; 3 dc in each rem sc; join in 3rd ch of beg ch-3.

Fasten off and weave in all ends.

Tie

Make chain about 1¾ yds in length or desired length. Fasten off and weave in ends.

Finishing

Beg at center of front, thread tie through row 2 of Upper Front and Upper Back. Attach 1 ball button to each end of Tie. Tie into bow. ❑❑

Sunshine Poncho

Design by Maria Cook for Coats & Clark

SKILL LEVEL

INTERMEDIATE

FINISHED SIZE
One size fits most

MATERIALS
- ❏ Aunt Lydia's Double Strand size 3 crochet cotton (300 yds per ball):
    - 2 balls #460 golden yellow/pumpkin
- ❏ Aunt Lydia's Classic Crochet size 10 crochet cotton (350 yds per ball):
    - 1 ball each #422 golden yellow and #431 pumpkin
- ❏ Sizes B/1/2.25 and D/3/3.25mm crochet hooks or sizes needed to obtain gauge
- ❏ Tapestry needle
- ❏ Sewing needle and matching thread
- ❏ 12 pearl beads, 1/16-inch in diameter

GAUGE
Size D hook and double strand:
8 ch-5 sps= 4 inches

INSTRUCTIONS

Poncho

Rnd 1 (RS): With D hook and double strand, ch 202; join with sl st to form a ring; ch 5 *(counts as a dc and a ch-2 on this and following rnds)*, dc in same ch as joining and in next 100 chs; in next ch work (dc, ch 2, dc); dc in each rem ch; join with sl st in 3rd ch of beg ch-5. *(204 dc)*

Rnd 2: Sl st in next ch-2 sp; ch 5, dc in same sp and in each dc to next ch-2 sp; in ch-2 sp work (dc, ch 2, dc); dc in each rem dc and in joining sl st; join with sl st in 3rd ch of beg ch-5. *(208 dc)*

Rnd 3: Rep rnd 2. *(212 dc)*

Rnd 4: Sl st in next ch-2 sp, ch 1, sc in same sp; ch 5, sk next 2 dc, [sc in next dc, ch 5, sk next 2 dc] 35 times; sc in next ch-2 sp, ch 5, sk

next 2 dc, [sc in next dc, ch 5, sk next 2 dc] 35 times; join with sl st in first sc. *(72 ch-5 sps)*

Rnd 5: Sl st in next sp; ch 1, sc in same sp; ch 5; *sc in next ch-5 sp, ch 5; rep from * around; join with sl st in first sc.

Rnds 6–9: Rep rnd 5.

Rnd 10: Sl st in next ch-5 sp, ch 3 *(counts as a dc on this and following rnds)*, 3 dc in same sp; 4 dc in each of next 33 ch-5 sps; in next ch-5 sp work (3 dc, ch 1, 3 dc); 4 dc in each of next 35 sps; in next ch-5 sp work (3 dc, ch 1, 3 dc); 4 dc in last ch-5 sp; join with sl st in 3rd ch of beg ch-3. *(292 dc)*

Rnd 11: Ch 3, dc in same ch as joining and in next 3 dc, [2 dc in next dc, dc in next 3 dc] 33 times; 2 dc in next dc; dc in next 2 dc, in next sp work (dc, ch 1, dc); 2 dc in next dc; dc in next 2 dc, [2 dc in next dc, dc in next 3 dc] 35 times; 2 dc in next dc; dc in next 2 dc, in next sp work (dc, ch 1, dc); 2 dc in next dc; dc in next 2 dc, 2 dc in next dc; dc in last 3 dc; join with sl st in 3rd ch of beg ch-3. *(370 dc)*

Rnd 12: Ch 2, dc in next 2 dc, **dc dec** *(see Stitch Guide)* in next 2 dc; ch 1, [dc dec in next 2 dc, dc in next dc, dc dec in next 2 dc, ch 1] 33 times; dc dec in next 2 dc; dc in next dc, dc dec in next 2 dc; ch 3, dc dec in next 2 dc; dc in next dc, dc dec in next 2 dc; ch 1, [dc dec in next 2 dc, dc in next dc, dc dec in next 2 dc, ch 1] 35 times; dc dec in next 2 dc; dc in next dc, dc dec in next 2 dc; ch 3, dc dec in next 2 dc; dc in next dc, dc dec in next 2 dc; ch 1, dc dec in next 2 dc; dc in next dc, dc dec in next 2 dc; ch 1; join with sl st in first dc. *(72 ch-1 sps, 2 ch-3 sps)*

Rnd 13: Sl st in next 2 sts and in next sp, ch 1, sc in same sp; ch 5, [sc in next ch-1 sp, ch 5] 33 times; in next ch-3 sp work [sc, ch 5] 3 times; sc in next ch-1 sp, [ch 5, sc in next ch-1 sp] 35 times; ch 5, in next ch-3 sp work [sc, ch 5] 3 times; sc in next ch-1 sp, ch 5, sc in next ch-1 sp, ch 5; join with sl st in first sc. *(78 ch-5 sps)*

Rnd 14: Sl st in next ch-5 sp; ch 1, sc in same sp; ch 5; *sc in next sp, ch 5; rep from * around; join with sl st in first sc.

Rnds 15–19: Rep rnd 14.

Rnd 20: Sl st in next ch-5 sp; ch 3, 4 dc in same sp; ch 1; *5 dc in next ch-5 sp, ch 1; rep from * around; join with sl st in 3rd ch of beg ch-3. *(390 dc)*

Rnd 21: Ch 3, dc in next 4 dc, [dc in ch-1 sp and in next 5 dc] 31 times; in next ch-1 sp work (2 dc, ch 3, 2 dc); dc in next 5 dc, [dc in next sp, dc in next 5 dc] 38 times; in next ch-1 sp work (2 dc, ch 3, 2 dc); [dc in next 5 dc, dc in next sp] 7 times; join with sl st in 3rd ch of beg ch-3. *(474 dc)*

Rnd 22: Ch 3, dc dec in next 2 dc; dc in next dc, dc dec in next 2 dc; ch 1, [{dc in next dc, dc dec in next 2 dc} twice, ch 1] 30 times; [dc in next dc, dc dec in next 2 dc] twice; dc in next dc, in next sp work (2 dc, ch 3, 2 dc); [dc in next dc, dc dec in next 2 dc] twice; dc in next dc, ch 1, [{dc in next dc, dc dec in next 2 dc} twice; ch 1] 37 times; dc dec in next 2 dc, [dc in next dc, dc dec in next 2 dc] twice; (2 dc, ch 3, 2 dc) in next sp; dc dec in next 2 dc, [dc in next dc, dc dec in next 2 dc] twice; ch 1, [{dc in next dc, dc dec in next 2 dc} twice, ch 1] 6 times; join with sl st in 3rd ch of beg ch-3. *(76 ch-1 sps, 2 ch-3 sps)*

Rnd 23: Sl st in next 2 sts, ch 1, sc in same st as last sl st made; ch 5, sc in next sp, [ch 5, sk 2 sts, sc in next st, ch 5, sc in next sp] 30 times; [ch 5, sk 2 sts, sc in next st] twice; ch 5, in next ch-3 sp work (dc, ch 3, dc); ch 5, sk next dc, sc in next dc, [ch 5, sk 2 sts, sc in next st, ch 5, sc in next sp] 38 times; [ch 5, sk 2 sts, sc in next st] twice; ch 5, in next ch-3 sp work (dc, ch 3, dc); ch 5, sk next dc, sc in next dc, [ch 5, sk 2 sts, sc in next st, ch 5, sc in next sp] 7 times; ch 5; join with sl st in first sc. *(160 ch-5 sps, 2 ch-3 sps)*

Rnd 24: Sl st in next ch-5 sp; ch 1, sc in same sp; *ch 5, [sc in next ch-5 sp, ch 5] to next ch-3 sp; in ch-3 sp work (dc, ch 3, dc); rep from * once; ch 5; **sc in next ch-5 sp, ch 5; rep from ** to first sc; join with sl st in first sc.

Rnds 25–48: Rep rnd 24.

Rnd 49: Sl st in next ch-5 sp; ch 1, in same sp and in each rem ch-5 sp work (sc, ch 2, 4 dc) and in each ch-3 sp work (sc, 5 dc, sc); join with sl st in first sc.

Fasten off and weave in ends.

Neck Edging

Hold piece with RS facing you and neck opening at top; with D hook, join A in any unused lp of beg ch; ch 1, sc in same lp; ch 3, working in rem unused lps of beg ch, *sk next lp, sc in next lp, ch 3; rep from * around; join with sl st in first sc.

Fasten off and weave in ends.

Flower
Make 6 each golden yellow & pumpkin.

Rnd 1: With B hook, ch 7; dc in 7th ch from hook *(beg 6 sk chs count as a dc and a ch-3 sp)*; ch 3, in same ch work [dc, ch 3] 4 times; join with sl st in 3rd ch of beg 6 sk chs. *(6 ch-3 sps)*

Rnd 2: Sl st in next ch-3 sp; in same sp and in each rem sp work (sc, hdc, 2 dc, hdc, sc)—*petal made*; join with sl st in first sc. *(6 petals)*

Rnd 3: Working behind petals made on last rnd, ch 4, [sl st in next dc of rnd 1, ch 4] 5 times, join with sl st in joining sl st. *(6 ch-4 sps)*

Rnd 4: Sl st in next ch-4 sp; in same sp and in each rem ch-4 sp work (sc, hdc, 4 dc, hdc, sc); join with sl st in first sc.

Fasten off and weave in ends.

Finishing

With sewing needle and matching thread, sew Flowers, evenly spaced along rnd 2, alternating colors. Sew 1 pearl bead to center of each Flower. ❑❑

Splash 'n' Fun Swimsuit & Cover-Up

Designs by Jenny King

SKILL LEVEL

INTERMEDIATE

FINISHED SIZES

Instructions given fit girl's size 2–3; changes for size 4–5 are in [ ].

FINISHED GARMENT MEASUREMENTS

Cover-Up: 12½ [14] inches around chest.
Swimsuit: 16 [18] inches long

MATERIALS

- ❑ Size 3 crochet cotton:
    150 yds each white and red
- ❑ Size D/3/3.25mm crochet hook or size needed to obtain gauge
- ❑ Tapestry needle
- ❑ 2 yds ⅛-inch elastic
- ❑ 2 plastic 1-inch rings
- ❑ Sewing needle and matching thread

GAUGE

7 ch-5 sps and 7 sc = 4 inches
5 shells and 5 sc = 4 inches

SPECIAL STITCHES

Beginning shell (beg shell): Ch 3, 2 dc in st indicated.
Shell (shell): 3 dc in st indicated.

INSTRUCTIONS
COVER-UP

Rnd 1: With white, ch 5; dc in 5th ch from hook, [ch 5, dc in last dc made] 4 times; ch 5, sc in last dc made—*corner made;* ch 5, dc in last sc made—*sleeve made;* [ch 5, dc in last dc made] 6 times; ch 5—*corner sp made;* sc in last dc, ch 5, dc in

Cover-Up

14½ (16¼)"

12½ (14)"

last sc made—*front made;* [ch 5, dc in last dc made] 9 times; ch 5, sc in last dc made—*corner made;* ch 5, dc in last sc made—*sleeve made;* [ch 5, dc in last dc made] 6 times; ch 5, sc in last dc made—*corner made;* [ch 5, dc in last dc made] 5 times; join with sl st in unused lp of same ch as first dc worked. *(38 ch sps)*

Rnd 2: Sl st in next 2 chs of beg 4 sk chs on rnd 1, ch 1, sc in sp formed by same beg chs; *ch 5, in each ch-5 sp to next corner ch-2 sp work (sc, ch 5); in corner ch-2 sp work (sc, ch 5, sc)—*corner made;* rep from * 3 times; ch 5, in each ch-5 sp to last ch-5 sp work (sc, ch 5); sc in last ch-5 sp, ch 2; join with a dc in first sc. *(42 sc)*

Rnd 3: Ch 1, sc in sp formed by joining dc; *ch 5, in each ch-5 sp to next corner ch-5 sp work (sc, ch 5); in corner ch-5 sp work corner; rep from * 3 times; ch 5, in each ch-5 sp to last ch-5 sp work (sc, ch 5); sc in last ch-5 sp; join with a dc in first sc.

Rnds 4–11 [4–13]: Rep rnd 3. *(78 [86] ch-5 sps at end of last row)*

For Size 2-3 Only

Rnd 12: Ch 1, sc in sp formed by joining dc, ch 5, [sc in next ch-5 sp, ch 5] 15 [17] times; sk next 17 [19] ch-5 sps—*armhole made;* [sc in next ch-5 sp, ch 5] 22 [24] times; sk next 17 [19] ch-5 sps—*armhole made;* sc in next ch-5 sp, [ch 5, sc in next ch-5 sp] 5 times; join with a dc in first sc.

Rnd 13: Ch 1, sc in sp formed by joining dc; *ch 5, sc in next ch-5 sp; rep from * around; join with a dc in first sc.

For Both Sizes

Rnds 14–49 [14–55]: Rep rnd 13.

Rnd 50 [56]: Ch 1, sc in sp formed by joining dc, ch 5; *sc in next ch-5 sp, ch 5; rep from * around; join with sl st in first sc.

Rnd 51 [57]: Ch 1, 3 sc in each ch-5 sp; join with sl st in first sc.

Rnd 52 [58]: Ch 1, working in **back**

lps *(see Stitch Guide)* only, sc in same sc and in each rem sc; join with sl st in first sc. Fasten off.

Armhole Edging

Rnd 1: Working in unworked ch-5 sps of 1 armhole, with white, make slip knot on hook and join with sc in first ch-5 sp; 2 sc in same sp; 3 sc in each rem ch-5 sp; join with sl st in first sc.

Rnd 2: Ch 1, working in back lps only, sc in same sc and in each rem sc; join with sl st in first sc. Fasten off.

Rep on other armhole

Hood

Row 1: Hold piece with neck opening at top; working in sps formed by dc on rnd 1, with white, make slip knot on hook and join with sc in sp formed by 6th dc of front; *ch 5, sc in sp formed by next dc; rep from * to last dc; ch 2, dc in last dc, turn. *(33 ch sps)*

Row 2: Ch 5, sk next ch-2 sp, [sc in next ch-5 sp, ch 5] 15 times; in next ch-5 sp work (sc, ch 5, sc); [ch 5, sc in next ch-5 sp] 15 times; ch 2, dc in last ch-5 sp, turn.

Rows 3–5: Rep row 2.

Row 6: Ch 5, sk next ch-2 sp, sc in next ch-5 sp; *ch 5, sc in next ch-5 sp; rep from * to last ch-5 sp; ch 2, dc in last ch-5 sp, turn. *(32 ch sps)*

Rows 7 & 8: Rep row 6. *(30 sps at end of row 8)*

Row 9: Ch 5, sk next ch-2 sp, sc in next ch-5 sp; *ch 5, sc in next ch-5 sp; rep from * across, turn. *(29 ch sps)*

Row 10: Ch 5, sc in next ch-5 sp, *ch 5, sc in next ch-5 sp; rep from * to last ch sp; ch 5, in last ch sp work (sc, ch 2, dc), turn. *(30 ch sps)*

Rows 11–24: [Work rows 9 and 10] 7 times.

Row 25: Ch 5, sk next ch-2 sp, sc in next ch-5 sp, [ch 5, sc in next ch-5 sp] 13 times; sc in next ch-5 sp, [ch 5, sc in next ch-5 sp] 13 times; ch 2, dc in last ch-5 sp, turn. *(28 ch sps)*

Row 26: Ch 5, sk next ch-2 sp, sc in next ch-5 sp, [ch 5, sc in next ch-5 sp] 12 times; sc in next ch-5 sp, [ch

5, sc in next ch-5 sp] 12 times; ch 5, in last ch-5 sp work (sc, ch 2, dc), turn. *(27 ch sps)*

Row 27: Ch 5, sk next ch-2 sp, sc in next ch-5 sp, [ch 5, sc in next ch-5 sp] 12 times; sc in next ch-5 sp, [ch 5, sc in next ch-5 sp] 11 times; ch 5, in last ch-5 sp work (sc, ch 2, dc), turn. *(26 ch sps)*

Row 28: Ch 5, sc in next ch-2 sp, [ch 5, sc in next ch-5 sp] 12 times; sc in next ch-5 sp, [ch 5, sc in next ch-5 sp] 11 times; ch 5, in last ch sp work (sc, ch 2, dc), turn.

Row 29: Ch 5, sk next ch-2 sp, sc in next ch-5 sp; *ch 5, sc in next ch-5 sp; rep from * across, turn.

Row 30: Ch 5, sc in next ch-5 sp; *ch 5, sc in next ch-5 sp; rep from * to last ch sp; ch 5, in last ch sp work (sc, ch 2, dc), turn. *(26 ch sps)*

Row 31: Rep row 29.

Joining row: Fold last row in half; ch 5, sc in first ch sp on other side, ch 5, sc in first ch sp on this side; *ch 5, sc in next ch sp on other side, ch 5, sc in next ch sp on this side; rep from * across.

Fasten off and weave in ends.

Hood Edging

Rnd 1: Hold Hood with RS facing you; working in ends of rows around Hood, with white make slip knot on hook and join with sc in end of first row; sc evenly around, keeping edge flat; join with sl st in back lp of first sc.

Rnd 2: Ch 1, working in back lps only, sc in same sc and in each rem sc; join with sl st in first sc.

Fasten off and weave in ends.

BATHING SUIT

Row 1: Starting at crotch and with red, ch 10; sc in 2nd ch from hook; *sk next ch, **shell** *(see Special Stitches)* in next ch; sk next ch, sc in next ch; rep from * across, turn. *(3 sc, 2 shells)*

Row 2: Beg shell *(see Special Stitches)* in first sc; *sc in center dc of next shell, shell in next sc; rep from * across, turn. *(3 shells, 2 sc)*

Row 3: Ch 1, sk first st, sc in next st; *shell in next sc, sc in center dc of next shell; rep from * across, turn.

Rows 4–9: [Work rows 2 and 3] 3 times.

Row 10: Rep row 2.

Row 11: For front, beg shell, sc in next st; *shell in next sc, sc in center dc of next shell; rep from * to last st; shell in last st, turn. *(4 shells, 3 sc)*

Row 12: Rep row 3.

Row 13: Rep row 2.

Row 14: Beg shell, sc in next st; *shell in next sc, sc in center dc of next shell; rep from * to last st; shell in last st, turn.

Rows 15–19 [15–21]: Rep row 14. *(10 shells and 9 sc [12 shells and 11 sc] at end of last row)*

Row 20 [22]: Beg shell, sc in next st, [shell in next sc, sc in center dc of next shell] 4 [5] times; sc in next sc, sc in center dc of next shell, [shell in next sc, sc in center dc of next shell] 4 [5] times; shell in last st, turn. *(11 sc, 10 shells [13 sc, 12 shells])*

Row 21 [23]: Beg shell, sc in next st, [shell in next sc, sc in center dc of next shell] 4 [5] times; sk next st, shell in next st; sk next st, sc in center dc of next shell, [shell in next sc, sc in center dc of next shell] 4 [5] times; shell in last st, turn. *(11 shells, 10 sc [13 shells, 12 sc])*

For Size 2-3 Only
Row 22: Beg shell, sc in next st, *shell in next sc, sc in center dc of next shell; rep from * to last st; shell in last st, turn.

For Both Sizes
Rows 23 & 24 [24–26]: Rep row 22. *(14 shells and 13 sc [16 shells and 15 sc] at end of last row)*

Row 25 [27]: Beg shell, sc in next st, shell in next sc, sc in center dc of next shell, [ch 5, sc in center dc of next shell] twice; *shell in next sc, sc in center dc of next shell; rep from * to last st, turn. *(14 sc, 13 shells, 2 ch-5 sps [16 sc, 15 shells, 2 ch-5 sps])*

Row 26 [28]: Ch 1, sk first st, sc in next st, [shell in next sc, sc in center dc of next shell] 10 [12] times; ch 5, sc in next ch sp, shell in next sc; sc in next ch sp, ch 5, sc in center dc of next shell, shell in next sc; sc in center dc of last shell, turn. *(15 sc, 12 shells, 2 ch-5 sps [17 sc, 14 shells, 2 ch-5 sps])*

Row 27 [29]: Ch 1, sc in center dc of next shell, shell in next sc; sc in next ch sp, ch 5, sc in center dc of next shell, ch 5, sc in next ch sp, [shell in next sc, sc in center dc of next shell] 10 [12] times, turn, leaving rem sts unworked. *(14 sc, 11 shells, 2 ch-5 sps [16 sc, 13 shells, 2 ch-5 sps])*

Row 28 [30]: Ch 1; *sc in center dc of next shell, shell in next sc; rep from * to next ch sp; [sc in next ch sp, shell in next sc] twice; sc in center dc of next shell, turn, leaving rem sts unworked. *(13 sc, 12 shells [15 sc, 14 shells])*

Row 29 [31]: Ch 1, sc in center dc of next shell; *shell in next sc, sc in center dc of next shell; rep from * to last sc, turn, leaving last sc unworked.
Row 30 [32]: Rep row 29 [31]. *(11 sc, 10 shells [13 sc, 12 shells])*
Row 31 [33]: Beg shell, sc in center dc of next shell, shell in next sc, sc in center dc of next shell, [ch 5, sc in center dc of next shell] twice; shell in next sc; *sc in center dc of next shell,

shell in next sc; rep from * across, turn. *(10 sc, 9 shells, 2 ch-5 sps [12 sc, 11 shells, 2 ch-5 sps])*

Row 32 [34]: Ch 1, sk first st, sc in next st, [shell in next sc, sc in center dc of next shell] 6 [8] times; ch 5, sc in next ch sp, shell in next sc; sc in next ch sp, ch 5, sc in center dc of next shell, shell in next sc, sc in center dc of last shell, turn. *(11 sc, 8 shells, 2 ch-5 sps [13 sc, 10 shells, 2 ch-5 sps])*

Row 33 [35]: Ch 1, sc in center dc of next shell, shell in next sc; sc in next ch sp, ch 5, sc in center dc of next shell, ch 5, sc in next ch sp; *shell in next sc; sc in center dc of next shell; rep from * to last sc, turn, leaving last sc unworked. *(10 sc, 7 shells, 2 ch-5 sps [12 sc, 9 shells, 2 ch-5 sps])*

Row 34 [36]: Ch 1; *sc in center dc of next shell, shell in next sc; rep from * to next ch sp; [sc in next ch sp, shell in next sc] twice; sc in center dc of last shell, turn, leaving rem sts unworked. *(9 sc, 8 shells [11 sc, 10 shells])*

For Size 2–3 Only
Continue with For All Sizes.

For Size 4–5 Only
Row 37: Ch 1, sc in center dc of next shell; *shell in next sc, sc in center dc of next shell; rep from * to last sc, turn, leaving last sc unworked, turn.

Row 38: Rep row 37. *(9 sc and 8 shells)*

For All Sizes
Row 35 [39]: Beg shell; *sc in center dc of next shell, shell in next sc; rep from * across, turn. *(9 shells, 8 sc)*

Row 36 [40]: Ch 1, sk first st, sc in next st; *shell in next sc, sc in center dc of next shell; rep from * across, turn. *(9 sc, 8 shells)*

Rows 37–42 [41–48]: Rep rows 35 and 36 [39 and 40] 3 [4] times.

Row 43 [49]: Rep row 35 [39].

Row 44 [50]: Beg shell; sc in next st; *shell in next sc; sc in center dc of next shell; rep from * to last st; shell in last st, turn.

Rows 45–49 [51–57]: Rep row 44 [50]. *(15 shells and 14 sc [17 shells and 16 sc] at end of last row)*

Row 50 [58]: Beg shell; sc in next st, [shell in next sc, sc in center dc of next shell] 6 [7] times; [ch 5, sc in center dc of next shell] twice; [shell in next sc, sc in center dc of next shell] 6 [7] times; shell in last st, turn. *(15 sc, 14 shells and 2 ch-5 sps [17 sc, 16 shells and 2 ch-5 sps])*

Row 51 [59]: Ch 1, sk first st, sc in next st, [shell in next sc, sc in center dc of next shell] 6 [7] times; ch 5, sc in next ch sp, shell in next sc; sc in next ch sp, ch 5, sc in center dc of next shell, [shell in next sc, sc in center dc of next shell] 6 [7] times, turn. *(16 sc, 13 shells and 2 ch-5 sps [18 sc, 15 shells and 2 ch-5 sps])*

Row 52 [60]: Ch 1, [sc in center dc of next shell, shell in next sc] 6 [7] times; sc in next ch sp, ch 5, sc in center dc of next shell, ch 5, sc in next ch sp, [shell in next sc, sc in center dc of next shell] 6 [7] times, turn, leaving last sc unworked. *(15 sc, 12 shells and 2 ch-5 sps [17 sc, 14 shells and 2 ch-5 sps])*

Row 53 [61]: Ch 1, [sc in center dc of next shell, shell in next sc] 6 [7] times; sc in next ch sp, shell in next sc; sc in next ch sp, [shell in next sc, sc in center dc of next shell] 6 [7] times, turn, leaving last sc unworked. *(14 sc and 13 shells [16 sc and 15 shells])*

Row 54 [62]: Ch 1, sc in center dc of next shell; *shell in next sc; sc in center dc of next shell; rep from * to last sc, turn, leaving last sc unworked.

Rows 55–58 [63–66]: Rep row 54 [62]. *(9 sc and 8 shells [11 sc and 10 shells] at end of last row)*

Row 59 [67]: Ch 1, sc in center dc of next shell; *ch 5, sc in center dc of next shell; rep from * to last sc. Fasten off, leaving last sc unworked.

Pants Back

Row 1: Hold piece with beg ch at top; join red in unused lp of first ch; beg shell; working in rem unused lps of beg ch, *sk next lp, sc in next lp, sk next lp, shell in next lp; rep from * across, turn. *(3 shells, 2 sc made)*

Row 2: Beg shell; sc in next st; *shell in next sc; sc in center dc of next shell; rep from * to last st; shell in last st, turn.

Rows 3–9 [3–11]: Rep row 2. *(11 shells and 10 sc [13 shells and 12 sc] at end of last row)*

Row 10 [12]: Ch 1, sk first st, sc in next st; *shell in next sc; sc in center dc of next shell; rep from * across, turn. *(11 sc and 10 shells [13 sc and 12 shells])*

Row 11 [13]: Beg shell; *sc in center dc of next shell, shell in next sc; rep from * across, turn. *(11 shells and 10 sc [13 shells and 12 sc])*

Rows 12–14 [14–16]: Rep row 2. *(14 shells and 13 sc [16 shells and 15 sc] at end of last row)*

Row 15 [17]: Rep row 10 [12]. *(14 sc and 13 shells [16 sc and 15 shells])*

Row 16 [18]: Ch 1, sc in center dc of next shell; *shell in next sc; sc in center dc of next shell; rep from * to last sc, turn, leaving last sc unworked; for first leg opening, ch 5, sl st in end of row 25 [27] on same side edge of front. Fasten off.

For 2nd leg opening, join red with sl st in other end of this row; ch 5, sl st in end of row 25 [27] on opposite side edge of front.

Fasten off and weave in ends.

Leg Opening Trim

Note: *Cut 2 pieces of elastic, each 13 inches long. Overlap ends of 1 piece ½ inch; sew tog forming ring. Rep with other piece.*

Working around 1 ring of elastic *(see illustration)* in sts and ends of rows around 1 leg opening, with red make slip knot on hook and join with sc in first row on crotch; work 99 [107] sc evenly spaced around opening; join with sl st in first sc.

Sc Around Elastic

Fasten off and weave in ends.
Rep on other leg opening.

Back Opening Trim

Note: *Cut 36-inch [44-inch] piece of elastic. Overlap ends ½ inch; sew tog forming ring.*

Working around elastic in sts and in ends of rows around outer edge of back opening, with RS of work facing you, with red make slip knot on hook and join with sc in first ch on right leg opening; sc evenly spaced around, spacing sc so piece lays flat; join with sl st in first sc.

Fasten off and weave in ends.

Tie
Make 2.

With red, ch 100 or to desired length. Fasten off and weave in ends.

Sew to center front edge of Swimsuit 3 inches apart (see photo).

For each plastic ring, with red make slip knot on hook and join with sc around 1 plastic ring; sc around ring until completely covered, join with sl st in first sc. Fasten off and weave in ends.

Sew 1 ring to top edge of Suit 2½ inches from each tie. ❑❑

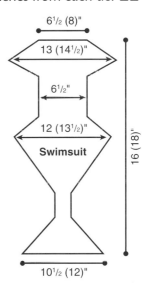

Iridescent Midnight Shawl

Design by Ferosa Harold

SKILL LEVEL

INTERMEDIATE

FINISHED SIZE

33 inches wide, excluding tie

MATERIALS

- ❑ Size 10 crochet cotton:
  1,000 yds navy
- ❑ Size 8/1.50mm steel crochet hook
  or size needed to obtain gauge
- ❑ 836 iridescent 8mm rice beads
- ❑ 2 silver 8mm-wide metal hair
  beads (the kind you squeeze
  tog around a section of hair)

GAUGE

9 sc = 1 inch

SPECIAL STITCH

Beaded chain (bch): Slide bead
up, ch 1.

INSTRUCTIONS

Shawl

Note: *String all rice beads on crochet
cotton.*

Row 1: Ch 503; dc in 4th ch from hook
(beg 3 sk chs count as a dc) and in
each rem ch, turn. *(501 dc)*

Row 2: Sl st in first 100 dc, ch 1, sc in
next dc, [**bch** *(see Special Stitch)*, ch 3,
bch, ch 5, bch, ch 3, bch, sk next 14
sts, sc in next st] 20 times, turn, leaving
rem sts unworked. *(20 bch lps)*

Row 3: Ch 5, sc in next ch-3 sp between
beads, ch 6, sc in next ch-5 sp between
beads; *ch 2, bch, ch 3, bch, ch 5,
bch, ch 3, bch, ch 2, sc in next ch-5
sp; rep from * across, turn.

Rows 4–19: Rep row 3.

Row 20: Ch 5, sc in next ch-3 sp
between beads, ch 6, sc in next ch-5
sp between beads, [ch 2, bch, ch 3,
bch, ch 5, bch, ch 3, bch, ch 2, sc
in next ch 5 sp] twice.

Fasten off and weave in ends.

Tassel

Make 2.

Cut 45 strands, each 6 inches long. Tie
separate strand around center of all
strands held tog; fold in half. Bend 1
hair bead around all strands ¼ inch
from fold. Trim ends even.

Tie 1 Tassel to end of each Tie.

Fringe

Cut 12-inch strands. For each knot of
fringe, use 2 strands. Fold strands in
half, insert hook in 1 ch-5 sp, pull fold
through; pull ends through fold and
tighten knot. Tie knots in each rem
ch-5 sp across sides and bottom of
Shawl. Trim ends even. ❑❑

Flower-Power Accessories

Designs courtesy of Coats & Clark

FINISHED SIZES

Flower: approximately 3¼ inches in diameter

Cell-phone bag: approximately 4 x 7 inches open, excluding flower and strap

MATERIALS

❑ Moda Dea Sassy Stripes light (light worsted) weight yarn (1¾ oz/147 yds/50g per ball): 1 ball #6983 spring or #6946 crush or #6980 rave
❑ Sizes G/6/4mm and H/8/5mm crochet hooks or sizes needed to obtain gauge
❑ Tapestry needle
❑ Purchased flip-flops
❑ Chain with 1¾-inch diameter ring attached

GAUGE

With H hook, rnds 1–7 = 3¼ inches
With G hook, 8 sc = 2 inches

INSTRUCTIONS

NECKLACE

Flower

Rnd 1 (RS): Make lp over finger with yarn, leaving several inches hanging at 1 end; remove lp from finger, insert H hook in lp, yo, draw up lp to RS, ch 1, in ring work (2 sc, 2 hdc, 2 dc, 3 tr); ch 3, join with sl st in first sc. *(9 sts)*

Do not tighten lp.

Rnd 2: Holding unworked portion of lp behind sts of last rnd and working over it as each st of working rnd is worked, ch 1, sl st between first 2 sc, ch 3, sl st between next 2 hdc, ch 3, sl st between next 2 dc, ch 3, sl st between next 2 tr, ch 3, sl st in next ch-3 sp, ch 3; join with sl st in first ch-1. *(5 ch-3 sps)*

Rnd 3: In each ch-3 sp work (sl st, ch 1, 5 dc, sl st)—*petal made;* join with sl st in first ch-1. *(5 petals)*

Rnd 4: Ch 1; working behind petals of last rnd in ch-3 sps of rnd before last, *insert hook from WS to RS between 2nd and 3rd dc of next petal, yo, draw up lp to WS, complete sl st, ch 3; rep from * around; join with sl st in first ch-1. *(5 ch-3 sps)*

Rnd 5: In each ch-3 sp work (sl st, ch 1, 7 dc, sl st)—*medium petal made;* join with sl st in first ch-1 sp. *(5 medium petals)*

Rnd 6: Ch 1, working behind petals of last rnd in ch-3 sps of rnd before last, *insert hook from WS to RS between 3rd and 4th dc of next petal, yo, draw up lp to WS, complete sl st, ch 3; rep from * around; join with sl st in first ch-1. *(5 ch-3 sps)*

Rnd 7: In each ch-3 sp work (sl st, ch 1, 9 dc, sl st)—*large petal made;* join with sl st in first ch-1 sp. Fasten off. *(5 large petals)*

Finishing

Pull end to tighten center of Flower. With tapestry needle, secure end.

With tapestry needle and matching yarn, sew lower edges of sts of last rnd to ring on chain.

FLIP-FLOPS

Flower

Make 2.

Rnds 1–7: Rep rnds 1–7 of Flower for Necklace.

Finishing

Pull end to tighten center of Flower. With tapestry needle, secure end.

With tapestry needle and matching yarn, tack 1 Flower to center front of each Flip-Flop strap.

CELL-PHONE BAG

Row 1 (RS): With G hook, ch 2; 5 sc in 2nd ch from hook, turn. *(5 sc)*

Note: *Rem rows of Bag are worked in* **back lps** *(see Stitch Guide) only, unless otherwise stated.*

Row 2: Ch 1, 2 sc in first sc; sc in next sc, 3 sc in next sc; sc in next sc, 2 sc in last sc, turn. *(9 sc)*

Row 3: Ch 1, 2 sc in first sc; sc in each sc to center sc of next 3-sc group, 3 sc in center sc; sc in each rem sc to last sc; 2 sc in last sc, turn. *(13 sc)*

Rows 4–6: Rep row 3. *(25 sc at end of row 6)*

Row 7: Ch 1, **sc dec** *(see Stitch Guide)* in first 2 sc; sc in each sc to center sc of next 3-sc group, 3 sc in center sc; sc in each sc to last 2 sc, sc dec in last 2 sc, turn. *(25 sc)*

Rows 8–32: Rep row 7.

Row 33: Ch 1, sc dec in first 2 sc; sc in each sc to center sc of next 3-sc group, in center sc work (sc, ch 3, sc); sc in each rem sc to last 2 sc, sc dec in last 2 sc.

Fasten off and weave in ends.

Strap

With G hook, ch 101; sl st in 2nd ch from hook and in each rem ch.

Fasten off and weave in ends.

Flower

Rnds 1–7: With G hook, rep rnds 1–7 of Flower for Necklace.

Finishing

Fold straight end of Bag up 3½ inches. With tapestry needle and matching yarn, sew side seams. Tack 1 end of Strap to either side of Bag at top opening. Tack rem end of Strap to opposite side of Bag at top opening. Tack Flower to pointed end of Bag on RS. ❏❏

Sunshine & Lace

Design by Tammy Hildebrand

INTERMEDIATE

FINISHED SIZE

Approximately 36 x 54 inches

MATERIALS

❏ Red Heart Classic medium (worsted) weight yarn (3½ oz/198 yds/100g per skein):
  5 skeins #1 white
  1 skein each #730 grenadine, #48 teal and #230 yellow
❏ Size I/9/5.5mm crochet hook or size needed to obtain gauge
❏ Tapestry needle

GAUGE

Motif= 9½ x 9½ inches

SPECIAL STITCHES

Cross-stitch (X-st): Sk next st, dc in next st, ch 3, dc in sk st.

Joining cross-stitch (joining X-st): Sk next st, dc in next st, ch 1, drop lp from hook, insert hook in center ch of corresponding ch-3 on adjacent motif, pull dropped lp through, ch 1, dc in sk st.

Joining chain-3 space (joining ch-3 sp): Ch 1, drop lp from hook, insert hook in center ch of corresponding ch-3 sp on adjacent motif, pull dropped lp through, ch 1.

Joining chain-5 space (joining ch-5 sp): Ch 2, drop lp from hook, insert hook in center ch of corresponding ch-5 sp on adjacent motif, pull dropped lp through, ch 2.

INSTRUCTIONS

First Motif

Rnd 1 (RS): With yellow, ch 4; join to form a ring; ch 4 (*counts as a dc and a ch-1 sp on this and following rnds*), [dc in ring, ch 1] 11 times; join with sl st in 3rd ch of beg ch-4. Fasten off. (*12 dc*)

Rnd 2: With grenadine, make slip knot on hook and join with sc in any ch-1 sp; sc in next ch-1 sp, in next ch-1 sp work (dc, ch 3, dc)—*corner made;* *sc in next 2 ch-1 sps, in next ch-1 sp work (dc, ch 3, dc)—*corner made;* rep from * twice; join with sl st in first sc. Fasten off.

Rnd 3: Join teal in any corner ch-3 sp; ch 3 (*counts as a dc*), in same sp work (dc, ch 3, 2 dc)—*beg 2-dc corner made;* dc in next 4 sts; *in next corner ch-3 sp work (2 dc, ch 3, 2 dc)—*2-dc corner made;* dc in next 4 sts; rep from * twice; join with sl st in 3rd ch of beg ch-3. Fasten off.

Rnd 4: Working in sps between sts, with yellow, make slip knot on hook and join with sc between 3rd and 4th dc of any 4-dc group on any side, ch 3, sc in same sp; sk next 2 dc, in next sp work (sc, ch 3, sc); working over next ch-3 corner sp of rnd 3 in corner ch-3 sp of rnd 2 work (tr, ch 5, tr)—*tr corner made;* *[sk next 2 dc, in next sp work (sc, ch 3, sc)] 3 times; working over next ch-3 corner sp of rnd 3 in corner ch-3 sp of rnd 2 work (tr, ch 5, tr)—*tr corner made;* rep from * twice; sk next 2 dc, in next sp work (sc, ch 3, sc); join with sl st in first sc. Fasten off.

Rnd 5: With white, make slip knot on hook and join with sc in any corner ch-5 sp; 6 sc in same sp; 3 sc in each of next 3 ch-3 sps; *7 sc in next ch-5 sp; 3 sc in each of next 3 ch-3 sps; rep from * twice; join with sl st in first sc.

Rnd 6: Sl st in next 2 sc, ch 4, dc in same sc; in each of next 2 sts work (dc, ch 1, dc); sk next 2 sts, [in sp before next 3-sc group work (dc, ch 1, dc)] 3 times; in sp before next 7-sc group work (dc, ch 1, dc); *sk next 2 sts, in each of next 3 sts work (dc, ch 1, dc); sk next 2 sts, [in sp before next 3-sc group work (dc, ch 1, dc)] 3 times; in sp before next 7-sc group work (dc, ch 1, dc); rep from * twice; join with sl st in first sc. Fasten off.

Rnd 7: Join grenadine in any ch-1 corner sp; ch 5 (*counts as a dc and a ch-2 sp*), dc in same sp; [sc in next 2 dc, ch 1, sk next ch-1 sp] 6 times; sc in next 2 dc; *in next ch-1 sp work (dc, ch 2, dc); [sc in next 2 dc, ch 1, sk next ch-1 sp] 6 times; sc in next 2 sts; rep from * twice; join with sl st in 3rd ch of beg-ch 5. Fasten off.

Rnd 8: Join white in **back lp** (*see Stitch Guide*) of first ch of any ch-2 corner sp; ch 6 (*counts as a dc and a ch-3 sp on this and following rnds*), dc in next ch, dc in next 16 sts skipping ch-1 sps; *dc in next ch, ch 3, dc in next ch, dc in next 16 sts skipping ch-1 sps; rep from * twice; join with sl st in 3rd ch of beg ch-6.

Rnd 9: Sl st in next ch-3 sp; ch 6, in same sp work (dc, ch 5, dc, ch 3, dc); [X-st (*see Special Stitches*) in next 2 sts] 9 times; *in next ch-3 sp work (dc, ch 3, dc, ch 5, dc, ch 3, dc); [X-st in next 2 sts] 9 times; rep from * twice; join with sl st in 3rd ch of beg ch-6.

Fasten off and weave in ends.

2nd Motif

Referring to Assembly Diagram for placement, work same as rnds 1–8 of First Motif.

Rnd 9 (joining rnd): Sl st in next ch-3 sp, in same sp work (ch 6, dc, **joining ch-5 sp**—*see Special Stitches*, dc, **joining ch-3 sp**—*see Special Stitches*, dc); [**joining X-st** (*see Special Stitches*) in next 2 sts] 9 times; in next ch-3 sp work (dc, joining ch-3 sp, dc, joining ch-5 sp, dc, ch 3, dc); [X-st in next 2 sts] 9 times; *in next ch-3 sp work (dc, ch 3, dc, ch 5, dc, ch 3, dc); [X-st in next 2 sts] 9 times; rep from * once; join with sl st in 3rd ch of beg ch-6.

Fasten off and weave in ends.

Remaining Motifs

Referring to Assembly Diagram for placement, work rem motifs as for 2nd Motif joining to adjacent motifs in similar manner and making sure all 4-corner joinings are secure.

Border

Rnd 1: With white, make slip knot on hook and join with sc in any corner ch-5 sp; 2 sc in same sp; *in each ch-3 sp to next joining work (dc, ch 1, dc); tr in joining, in each ch-3 sp to next corner ch-5 sp work (dc, ch 1, dc); 3 sc in corner ch-5 sp; rep from * twice; in each ch-3 sp to next joining work (dc, ch 1, dc); tr in joining, in each ch-3 sp work (dc, ch 1, dc); join with sl st in first sc. Fasten off.

Rnd 2: With grenadine, make slip knot on hook and join with sc in first sc of any 3-sc corner; *sc in next 2 sc, [{ch 1, sk next ch-1 sp, sc in next 2 sts} to last ch-1 sp before next tr, ch 1, sk next ch-1 sp, sc in next st, ch 1, sk next tr, sc in next st] to last motif before 3-sc corner; sk next ch-1 sp, sc in next st, ch 1, sk next tr, sc in next st, [ch 1, sk next ch-1 sp, sc in next 2 sts] to 2nd sc of next 3-sc corner; sc in next sc; rep from * around, ending last rep without working last sc; join with sl st in first sc. Fasten off.

Rnd 3: Join white in back lp of center st of any corner; ch 3, in same lp work (dc, ch 2, 2 dc)—*beg corner made;* working in back lps only, dc in each st to center st of next corner skipping ch-1 sps; *in center st work (2 dc, ch 2, 2 dc)—*corner made;* dc in each st to center st of next corner skipping ch-1 sps; rep from * once more; in center st work (2 dc, ch 2, 2 dc)—*corner made;* dc in each st beg ch-3; join 3rd ch beg ch-3.

Rnd 4: Sl st in next ch-2 sp; ch 6, dc in same sp; (X-st in next 2 sts) to next corner ch-2 sp; *in corner ch-2 sp work (dc, ch 3, dc); (X-st in next 2 sts) to next ch-2 sp; rep from * around; join with sl st in 3rd ch of beg ch-6.

Fasten off and weave in ends. ❏❏

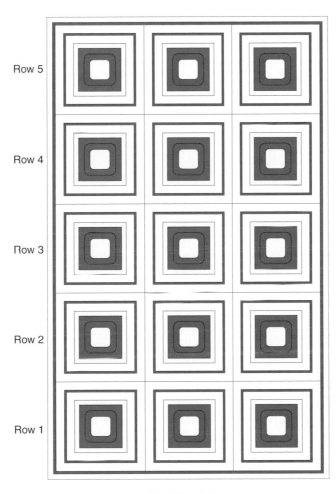

Sunshine & Lace
Assembly Diagram

Row 5

Row 4

Row 3

Row 2

Row 1

Daisy Tote-Along

Design by Sheila Leslie

FINISHED SIZE
2 inches deep x 10 inches tall x 11 inches wide

MATERIALS
❑ Brown Sheep Cotton Fleece light worsted (DK) weight yarn (3½ oz/215 yds/100g per ball):
2 balls #CW840 lime light
Small amount each of #CW830 sunburst and #CW100 cottonball
❑ Size H/8/5mm crochet hook or size needed to obtain gauge
❑ Tapestry needle
❑ Sewing needle and matching thread
❑ ¾-inch novelty button

GAUGE
4 dc= 1 inch

SPECIAL STITCH
Cross-stitch (X-st): Sk next st, dc in next st; working behind st just made, dc in sk st.

INSTRUCTIONS
Bag Side
Make 2.
Flower motif
Make 3.
Rnd 1 (RS): With sunburst, ch 4, join with sl st to form ring; ch 1, 8 sc in ring; join with sl st in first sc. Fasten off. *(8 sc)*
Rnd 2: Join cottonball with sl st in any sc; ch 4, in same st work (tr, ch 4, sl st)—*beg petal made;* in each rem sc work (sl st, ch 4, tr, ch 4, sl st)—*petal made;* join with sl st in joining sl st of last rnd. Fasten off. *(8 petals)*
Rnd 3: With lime light make slip knot on hook and join with sc in first tr; ch 4, sc in next tr, ch 5; *sc in next tr, ch 4, sc in next tr, ch 5; rep from * around; join with sl st in first sc. *(4 ch-4 sps, 4 ch-5 sps)*

Rnd 4: Ch 1, sc in same sc; 3 sc in next ch sp; sc in next st, in next ch sp work (2 sc, ch 3, 2 sc)—*corner made;* *sc in next st, 3 sc in next ch sp; sc in next st, in next ch sp work (2 sc, ch 3, 2 sc)—*corner made;* rep from * around; join with sl st in first sc. *(9 sc on each side between corner ch-3 sps)*
Rnd 5: Ch 1, sc in same sc and in each rem st and work (2 sc, ch 2, 2 sc) in each corner ch-3 sp; join with sl st in first sc. *(13 sc on each side between corner ch-3 sps)*
Fasten off and weave in ends.

Assembly
Join Motifs tog as follows. Working through both lps of first Motif and **back lps** *(see Stitch Guide)* of 2nd Motif and beg and ending in corner ch-3 sps, sew motifs tog along 1 side. Working through both lps of 2nd Motif and back lps of 3rd Motif; sew 3rd Motif to opposite side of 2nd Motif in same manner *(see photo).*

Bottom Section
Row 1: Hold joined motifs with RS facing you and 1 long edge at top, with lime light make slip knot on hook and join with sc in ch-3 sp in in upper right-hand corner; [sc in next 13 sc, sc in next ch-3 sps on either side of joining] twice; sc in next 13 sc, sc in next corner ch-3 sp, turn. *(45 sc)*
Row 2: Ch 1, sc in each sc, turn.
Rows 3 & 4: Rep row 2.
Row 5: Ch 3 *(counts as a dc)*, **X-st** *(see Special Stitch)* in next 2 sc; [X-st in next 2 sc] 21 times, turn.
Row 6: Ch 3, [X-st in next 2 dc] 22 times, turn.
Row 7: Rep row 6.
Row 8: Ch 1, sc in each dc, turn.
Rows 9–12: Rep row 9. At end of row 12, fasten off.

Top Section
Working on opposite side of long edge of joined Motifs, work same as Bottom Section.

Tab
Row 1: With lime light, ch 7; sc in 2nd ch from hook and in each rem ch, turn. *(6 sc)*
Row 2: Ch 1, sc in each sc, turn.
Rows 3–5: Rep row 2.
Row 6: Ch 1, sc in first 2 sc, ch 3—*buttonhole made,* sk next 2 sc; sc in last 2 sc, turn.
Row 7: Ch 1, sc in first sc, hdc in next sc, in next ch-3 sp work (dc, ch 3, sl st in 3rd ch from hook, dc); hdc in next sc, sc in last sc.
Fasten off and weave in ends.

Side Panel
Make 2.
Row 1: With lime light, ch 8; sc in 2nd ch from hook and in each rem ch, turn. *(7 sc)*
Row 2: Ch 1, sc in each sc, turn.
Rows 3–44 or number of rows needed to match height of Bag: Rep row 2. At end of last row, fasten off.

Bottom Panel
Work same as Side Panel to match width of Bag.

Assembly
Sew Side and Bottom Panels to Bag sides forming Bag.

Edging
Working around top edge of Bag, with lime light, make slip knot on hook and join with sc in any seam; working from left to right, work **reverse sc** *(see Stitch Guide)* in each st and in each seam; join with sl st in first sc.
Fasten off and weave in ends.

Handle
Make 2.
Row 1: With lime light, ch 6; sc in 2nd ch from hook and in each rem ch, turn. *(5 sc)*
Row 2: Ch 1, sc in each sc, turn.
Rows 3–117: Rep row 2.
Fasten off and weave in ends.

Finishing

Step 1: With tapestry needle and lime light, sew first row of Tab to center top edge of 1 Bag Side.

Step 2: With sewing needle and matching thread, sew button to top edge of other Bag Side opposite Tab.

Step 3: Referring to photo for placement and with tapestry needle and lime light, sew ends of 1 Handle to inside top edge of front, 5½ inches apart. Rep with other Handle on back. ❑❑

How to Check Gauge

A correct stitch gauge is very important. Please take the time to work a stitch gauge swatch about 4 x 4 inches. Measure the swatch. If the number of stitches and rows are fewer than indicated under "Gauge" in the pattern, your hook is too large. Try another swatch with a smaller-size hook. If the number of stitches and rows are more than indicated under "Gauge" in the pattern, your hook is too small. Try another swatch with a larger-size hook.

Abbreviations & Symbols

beg	beg/beginning
bpdc	back post double crochet
bpsc	back post single crochet
bptr	back post treble crochet
CC	contrasting color
ch	chain stitch
ch-	refers to chain or space previously made (i.e. ch-1 space)
ch sp	chain space
cl(s)	cluster(s)
cm	centimeter(s)
dc	double crochet
dec	decrease/decreases/decreasing
dtr	double treble crochet
fpdc	front post double crochet
fpsc	front post treble crochet
fptr	front post treble crochet
g	gram(s)
hdc	half double crochet
inc	increase/increases/increasing
lp(s)	loop(s)
MC	main color
mm	millimeter(s)
oz	ounce(s)
pc	popcorn
rem	remain/remaining
rep	repeat(s)
rnd(s)	round(s)
RS	right side
sc	single crochet
sk	skip(ped)
sl st	slip stitch
sp(s)	space(s)
st(s)	stitch(es)
tog	together
tr	treble crochet
trtr	triple treble crochet
WS	wrong side
yd(s)	yard(s)
yo	yarn over

* An asterisk is used to mark the beginning of a portion of instructions to be worked more than once; thus, "rep from * twice" means after working the instructions once, repeat the instructions following the asterisk twice more (3 times in all).

[ ] Brackets are used to enclose instructions that are to be worked the number of times indicated after the brackets. For example, "[2 dc in next st, sk next st] 5 times" means to follow the instructions within the brackets a total of 5 times.

( ) Parentheses are used to enclose a group of stitches that are worked in one space or stitch. For example, "(2 dc, ch 2, 2 dc) in next st" means to work all the stitches within the parentheses in the next space or stitch. Parentheses are also used to enclose special instructions or stitch counts.

Skill Levels

BEGINNER

Beginner projects for first-time crocheters using basic stitches. Minimal shaping.

EASY

Easy projects using basic stitches, repetitive stitch patterns, simple color changes and simple shaping and finishing.

INTERMEDIATE

Intermediate projects with a variety of stitches, mid-level shaping and finishing.

EXPERIENCED

Experienced projects using advanced techniques and stitches, detailed shaping and refined finishing.

Standard Yarn Weight System

Categories of yarn, gauge ranges, and recommended needle and hook sizes

Yarn Weight Symbol & Category Names	1 SUPER FINE	2 FINE	3 LIGHT	4 MEDIUM	5 BULKY	6 SUPER BULKY
Type of Yarns in Category	Sock, Fingering, Baby	Sport, Baby	DK, Light Worsted	Worsted, Afghan, Aran	Chunky, Craft, Rug	Super Chunky, Roving
Crochet Gauge* Ranges in Single Crochet to 4 inch	21–32 sts	16–20 sts	12–17 sts	11–14 sts	8–11 sts	5–9 sts
Recommended Hook in Metric Size Range	2.25–3.5 mm	3.5–4.5 mm	4.5–5.5 mm	5.5–6.5 mm	6.5–9 mm	9mm and larger
Recommended Hook U.S. Size Range	B-1–E-4	E-4–7	7–I-9	I-9–K-10½	K-10½–M-13	M-13 and larger

* GUIDELINES ONLY: The above reflect the most commonly used gauges and hook sizes for specific yarn categories.

Metric Chart

INCHES INTO MILLIMETERS & CENTIMETERS (Rounded off slightly)

inches	mm	cm	inches	cm	inches	cm	inches	cm
1/8	3	0.3	5	12.5	21	53.5	38	96.5
1/4	6	0.6	5 1/2	14	22	56	39	99
3/8	10	1	6	15	23	58.5	40	101.5
1/2	13	1.3	7	18	24	61	41	104
5/8	15	1.5	8	20.5	25	63.5	42	106.5
3/4	20	2	9	23	26	66	43	109
7/8	22	2.2	10	25.5	27	68.5	44	112
1	25	2.5	11	28	28	71	45	114.5
1 1/4	32	3.2	12	30.5	29	73.5	46	117
1 1/2	38	3.8	13	33	30	76	47	119.5
1 3/4	45	4.5	14	35.5	31	79	48	122
2	50	5	15	38	32	81.5	49	124.5
2 1/2	65	6.5	16	40.5	33	84	50	127
3	75	7.5	17	43	34	86.5		
3 1/2	90	9	18	46	35	89		
4	100	10	19	48.5	36	91.5		
4 1/2	115	11.5	20	51	37	94		

Stitch Guide

CROCHET HOOKS

Metric	US	Metric	US
.60mm	14	3.00mm	D/3
.75mm	12	3.50mm	E/4
1.00mm	10	4.00mm	F/5
1.50mm	6	4.50mm	G/6
1.75mm	5	5.00mm	H/8
2.00mm	B/1	5.50mm	I/9
2.50mm	C/2	6.00mm	J/10

Chain—ch: Yo, pull through lp on hook.

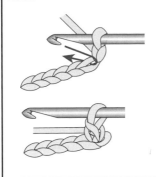

Slip stitch—sl st: Insert hook in st, yo, pull through both lps on hook.

Front loop—front lp
Back loop—back lp

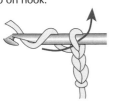

Front Loop   Back Loop

Single crochet—sc: Insert hook in st, yo, pull through st, yo, pull through both lps on hook.

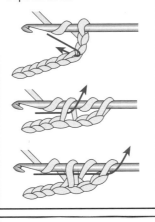

Reverse single crochet— reverse sc: Working from left to right, insert hook in next st, complete as sc.

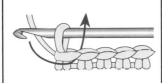

Front post stitch—fp: Back post stitch—bp: When working post st, insert hook from right to left around post st on previous row.

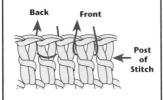

Back   Front

Post of Stitch

Half double crochet—hdc: Yo, insert hook in st, yo, pull through st, yo, pull through all 3 lps on hook.

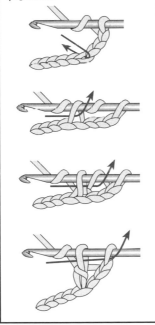

Double crochet—dc: Yo, insert hook in st, yo, pull through st, [yo, pull through 2 lps] twice.

Change colors: Drop first color; with second color, pull through last 2 lps of st.

Treble crochet—tr: Yo twice, insert hook in st, yo, pull through st, [yo, pull through 2 lps] 3 times.

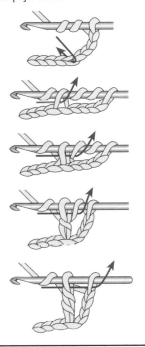

Double treble crochet— dtr: Yo 3 times, insert hook in st, yo, pull through st, [yo, pull through 2 lps] 4 times.

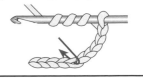

Single crochet decrease (sc dec): (Insert hook, yo, draw up a lp) in each of the sts indicated, yo, draw through all lps on hook.

Example of 2-sc dec

Half double crochet decrease (hdc dec): (Yo, insert hook, yo, draw lp through) in each of the sts indicated, yo, draw through all lps on hook.

Example of 2-hdc dec

Double crochet decrease (dc dec): (Yo, insert hook, yo, draw lp through, yo, draw through 2 lps on hook) in each of the sts indicated, yo, draw through all lps on hook.

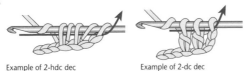

Example of 2-dc dec

US		UK
sl st (slip stitch)	=	sc (single crochet)
sc (single crochet)	=	dc (double crochet)
hdc (half double crochet)	=	htr (half treble crochet)
dc (double crochet)	=	tr (treble crochet)
tr (treble crochet)	=	dtr (double treble crochet)
dtr (double treble crochet)	=	ttr (triple treble crochet)
skip	=	miss

For more complete information, visit

AnniesAttic.com

306 East Parr Road
Berne, IN 46711
© 2006 Needlecraft Shop

TOLL-FREE ORDER LINE or to request a free catalog (800) LV-ANNIE (800) 582-6643
Customer Service (800) AT-ANNIE (800) 282-6643, **Fax** (800) 882-6643
Visit www.AnniesAttic.com

ISBN-10: 1-57367-248-3   ISBN-13: 978-1-57367-248-1